Press Office 3.0: Public Relations Strategies in the Era of Digital Cancellation

Copyright © 2024 Reginaldo Osnildo
All rights reserved.

PRESENTATION

INTRODUCTION TO PRESS OFFICE 3.0

UNDERSTANDING DIGITAL CANCELLATION

THE IMPORTANCE OF ONLINE REPUTATION

PROACTIVE PR STRATEGIES

DIGITAL MEDIA MONITORING

CRISIS COMMUNICATION IN THE DIGITAL AGE

MANAGING CANCELLATION ON SOCIAL MEDIA

ENGAGEMENT WITH INFLUENCERS

SEO FOR PUBLIC RELATIONS

BRANDED CONTENT AND STORYTELLING

MEDIA RELATIONSHIPS IN THE DIGITAL WORLD

STAKEHOLDER MANAGEMENT

TRANSPARENCY AND AUTHENTICITY

VISUAL CONTENT STRATEGIES

DIGITAL RIGHTS AND ONLINE ETHICS

EMERGING TECHNOLOGIES IN PR

DATA ANALYSIS IN PR

ONLINE FEEDBACK MANAGEMENT

PREVENTING DIGITAL CRISES

SPOKESKEEP TRAINING

MULTI-CHANNEL NARRATIVES

PR AND CORPORATE SOCIAL RESPONSIBILITY (CSR)

PR STRATEGIES FOR STARTUPS

PR CAMPAIGN DEVELOPMENT

THE FUTURE OF DIGITAL PUBLIC RELATIONS

REGINALDO OSNILDO

PRESENTATION

Welcome to a transformative journey through the dynamic and challenging world of digital public relations. As you venture through the pages of this book, you will delve into an invaluable source of practical strategies, deep insights, and tailored guidance for successfully navigating the contemporary digital environment.

This book is a compass for PR professionals, brands, and public figures seeking to not just survive, but thrive amid the turbulent waves of digital cancellation and the constant evolution of Web 3.0. Through a unique combination of up-to-date theory and practical applications, we offer you a comprehensive guide to building, managing and protecting your online reputation.

From crisis prevention and management to establishing an authentic and reputable digital presence, this book covers every crucial aspect you need to know to stand out in today's digital landscape. You will learn not only to face challenges, but to transform them into opportunities to strengthen your brand and your voice in the digital world.

Each chapter in this book has been carefully crafted to complement one another, offering a logical and engaging progression through the various themes. We will begin with an "**INTRODUCTION TO PRESS OFFICE 3.0**", where we will explore the evolution of public relations in the digital age and the emerging concept of digital cancellation. This chapter will serve as the foundation for all the knowledge you will build throughout the book.

As we progress, each chapter will not only delve into specific areas such as online reputation management, proactive PR strategies, digital media monitoring, and more, but will also invite you to explore the next chapter while continuing your learning journey. continuous and integrated.

This is not just a book; is a partner in your growth and success in the digital environment. By sharing my insights and syntheses of the most current knowledge, I hope to facilitate your journey, enabling you to not only adapt, but lead at the forefront of digital public relations.

Get ready to transform the way you see and interact with the digital world. Let's together uncover the secrets to building an unshakable online reputation, managing crises masterfully and taking advantage of the opportunities that the digital era offers.

Welcome to the future of public relations. Welcome to "**Press Office 3.0: Public Relations Strategies in the Era of Digital Cancellation**". The journey begins now.

Yours sincerely

Reginaldo Osnildo

INTRODUCTION TO PRESS OFFICE 3.0

As you enter the world of Press Relations 3.0, it is crucial to understand that the digital landscape we navigate today is not just a technological evolution, but a complete transformation in the way brands and public figures communicate with their audiences. This chapter offers an overview of the trajectory of public relations (PR) in the digital era, emphasizing the emerging phenomenon of digital cancellation and how it redefines PR strategies.

THE EVOLUTION OF PUBLIC RELATIONS IN THE DIGITAL AGE

Public relations, as you know, has its roots deeply embedded in the history of human communication. However, the rise of the internet and social media has radically transformed the field of PR. Today, we live in the era of Press Office 3.0, where the speed, interactivity and ubiquity of digital communication have reshaped the way brands interact with their audiences.

The digital era brought with it a new paradigm: the democratization of information. As a result, brands and public figures found themselves faced with the challenge and opportunity to communicate directly with their audience, without intermediaries. This scenario not only implies greater proximity and authenticity in communication, but also exposes brands to more intense and immediate public scrutiny.

THE EMERGENCE OF DIGITAL CANCELLATION

At the heart of this transformation is the concept of "digital cancellation". This phenomenon, characterized by rapid and broad mobilization against individuals or organizations in response to actions considered offensive or inappropriate, is one of the biggest challenges faced in the era of Press Office 3.0.

Digital unsubscription can have devastating impacts on a brand or public personality's online reputation, often with far-reaching financial and social consequences. Therefore, understanding this phenomenon is the first step to developing effective crisis management and online reputation strategies.

ADAPTING TO THE NEW REALITY

To successfully navigate this environment, it is essential to adapt traditional public relations strategies to the digital context. This means adopting a more dynamic and interactive approach, where active listening and rapid response become essential components of reputation management.

Furthermore, Press Office 3.0 requires a deep understanding of digital platforms and data analysis tools. These technologies allow you to not only monitor online presence and sentiment towards the brand, but also identify opportunities for proactive and personalized engagement with the public.

As you progress through this book, you will be equipped with the tools, strategies, and insights you need to face the challenges of digital unsubscribe and build a strong, resilient online reputation. The next chapter, " **UNDERSTANDING DIGITAL CANCELLATION** ", will delve deeper into this concept, exploring its causes, impacts and, most importantly, how you can prepare to prevent or respond to such crises.

Whether you're just beginning your public relations journey or looking to enhance your existing strategies for the digital environment, this book is your essential guide to Public Relations 3.0. I invite you to continue the journey with us as we together uncover the secrets to thriving in the age of digital cancellation.

UNDERSTANDING DIGITAL CANCELLATION

The phenomenon of digital cancellation, a reality increasingly present in the digital public relations scenario, represents one of the biggest challenges for brands, public figures and professionals in the field. In this chapter, we will dive deep into the concept of digital cancellation, understanding its nuances, impacts and, above all, how to prepare and respond to these delicate situations.

WHAT IS DIGITAL CANCELLATION?

Digital canceling refers to the practice of boycotting individuals, brands or companies after the publication of behavior, comments or actions considered offensive or inappropriate. This phenomenon is amplified by the speed and reach of social media, allowing cancellation campaigns to gain traction quickly and, often, with significant consequences for those involved.

Cancellation can arise from a variety of situations, from controversial statements in interviews or social media posts to the revelation of inappropriate behavior or controversial company policies. Regardless of the cause, the result is a rapid and often ruthless reaction from the public, impacting the reputation and, in many cases, the financial viability of the brand or public personality in question.

IMPACT OF DIGITAL CANCELLATION

The impact of digital cancellation goes beyond the simple loss of followers or a momentary drop in sales. It can profoundly affect public perception of the brand or personality, resulting in long-term reputational damage. This damage can manifest itself in several ways, including:

- **Consumer boycotts** : Significant reduction in customer loyalty and profits.

- **Devaluation of the brand** : Loss of market value and potential lack of interest from investors and partners.

- **Recruitment difficulties** : Complications in attracting and retaining talent due to a negative image.

Furthermore, digital cancellation can also have devastating effects on the emotional and psychological well-being of the individuals directly affected, exacerbating the severity of the phenomenon.

STRATEGIES FOR PREVENTION AND RESPONSE

While digital cancellation may seem like an invincible monster, there are effective strategies you can employ to minimize risks and respond constructively when faced with such challenges:

- **Constant monitoring** : Use social media monitoring tools to monitor what is being said about your brand or person in real time. This allows for a quick response to any sign of trouble.

- **Transparency and authenticity** : Be clear, honest and truthful in all your communications. This helps build trust with your audience and can mitigate negative impacts if something goes wrong.

- **Crisis response plans** : Develop a detailed crisis communication plan, preparing yourself to respond quickly and effectively to any cancellation situation. This includes having pre-approved messages and established communication channels.

- **Proactive engagement** : Maintain an open and ongoing dialogue with your audience. This not only strengthens the relationship with your follower base, but can also serve as a safety net, providing a channel for quick clarification and redress if necessary.

Understanding digital unsubscribe is the first step to developing a robust and resilient public relations strategy in the digital age. In the next chapter, " **THE IMPORTANCE OF ONLINE REPUTATION** ", we'll explore how to manage and protect your online reputation in an increasingly connected and visible world.

The journey to strengthen your digital presence and protect your brand against the headwinds of digital cancellation continues. Equipped with the right knowledge and strategies, you are prepared to face these challenges head-on and emerge even stronger. Let's move forward together on this journey, shaping a digital narrative that not only stands the test of time, but also thrives in the face of challenges.

THE IMPORTANCE OF ONLINE REPUTATION

In today's digital world, a brand or public personality's online reputation can be its most valuable asset or its greatest vulnerability. This chapter explores the fundamental importance of managing and protecting your online reputation, offering practical strategies for maintaining a positive image on the web.

UNDERSTANDING ONLINE REPUTATION

Your online reputation is the sum of the perceptions that the public has about your brand or personality, based on information available on the internet. This includes everything from comments on social media and reviews on review sites to news articles and blog posts. In a digital environment where information — both positive and negative — can spread quickly, maintaining a positive online reputation is crucial to your brand's success and survival.

WHY IS ONLINE REPUTATION CRUCIAL?

Online reputation directly impacts several aspects of your business or public career, including:

- **Consumer trust** : A positive reputation increases consumer trust, which is essential for retaining customers and attracting new ones.

- **Purchasing decisions** : Many consumers consult online reviews before making purchasing decisions, which means that a good reputation can directly increase your sales.

- **Perception of value** : A solid online reputation can improve the perception of your brand's value, allowing you to stand out from the competition.

- **Talent attraction** : Companies with positive reputations attract high-quality candidates, as people prefer to work for respected brands.

STRATEGIES TO MANAGE AND PROTECT YOUR REPUTATION ONLINE

- **Monitor your online presence** : Use monitoring tools to stay up to date with what is being said about your brand on the internet. This allows you to respond promptly to any negative feedback or false information.

- **Active engagement** : Maintain a constant dialogue with your audience. Respond to comments, both positive and negative, respectfully and constructively. This demonstrates that you value feedback and are committed to improving.

– **Quality content** : Regularly publish relevant and valuable content that reflects positively on your brand. This not only improves your reputation but also contributes to a stronger online presence.

- **Crisis management** : Have a crisis management plan ready to implement if a serious problem arises. A quick and effective response can minimize damage to your reputation.

- **Focus on transparency** : Be transparent in your operations and communications. Admitting mistakes and taking corrective action demonstrates integrity and can, paradoxically, improve public perception.

Maintaining a positive online reputation is an ongoing process that requires vigilance, dedication and strategy. In the next chapter, "**PROACTIVE PR STRATEGIES** ," we'll explore how to develop and implement proactive tactics to build and maintain a positive public image.

As you progress through this book, remember that every step you take to protect your online reputation is an investment in the future of your brand or public career. We invite you to follow us on this journey, armed with the knowledge and tools to not only respond to challenges, but anticipate them and transform them into opportunities to grow and strengthen your digital presence.

PROACTIVE PR STRATEGIES

Navigating the digital environment requires more than simply reacting to crises and negative feedback; demands a proactive approach to building and maintaining a positive public image. This chapter is dedicated to exploring proactive Public Relations (PR) strategies that can be used to strengthen your online presence, cultivate a robust brand image, and establish an authentic connection with your audience.

THE IMPORTANCE OF PROACTIVITY IN PR

A proactive PR strategy not only prepares you to manage crises, but also helps prevent them. By establishing a positive narrative and controlling the public perception of your brand, you can significantly influence how you are perceived online. This involves not only monitoring and responding to conversations about your brand, but also leading those conversations strategically.

DEVELOPING A PROACTIVE STRATEGY

To create an effective proactive approach to PR, consider the following elements:

- **Identification and understanding of the target audience** : Get to know your audience in depth. What are your preferences, online behaviors and preferred social media channels? This understanding allows you to create messages that resonate and engage your audience effectively.

- **Creating valuable content** : Produce and distribute content that is not only relevant, but also valuable to your audience. This can include informative articles, blog posts, videos, infographics, and case studies that position your brand as a thought leader in your industry.

- **Building relationships with the media** : Establish and maintain positive relationships with journalists, bloggers and influencers who can help spread your message in a positive way. This includes sending press releases about company news, innovative products or impactful research.

- **Engagement on social media** : Use social media to engage directly with your audience, promoting two-way communication. This helps build trust and loyalty, and allows you to actively shape public perception of your brand.

- **Monitoring and analysis** : Make use of monitoring tools to track what is being said about your brand online and evaluate the effectiveness of your PR strategies. This allows for quick, informed adjustments, ensuring your actions are aligned with your brand's goals.

IMPLEMENTING PROACTIVE STRATEGIES

With these strategies in hand, it's crucial to implement them consistently and adjust them as needed. Remember, PR proactivity is not a one-time task, but an ongoing process of engagement, assessment and adaptation.

As you move forward in building a proactive PR strategy, the next chapter, " **DIGITAL MEDIA MONITORING** ," will offer valuable insights into the tools and techniques needed to monitor your digital presence and identify potential crises before they escalate. This knowledge is critical for any PR professional looking to not only manage their online reputation, but also proactively strengthen it.

By equipping yourself with the right strategies and taking a proactive approach, you are not only protecting your brand against potential crises, but also positioning it for success in the digital environment. Stay with us on this journey as we explore more tools and techniques to ensure your brand or public persona flourishes in the digital age.

DIGITAL MEDIA MONITORING

In the current digital ecosystem, where information circulates with unprecedented speed and volume, digital media monitoring becomes an indispensable tool for any effective Public Relations (PR) strategy. This chapter covers the essential tools and techniques for monitoring your digital presence, allowing you to identify opportunities for positive engagement and potential crises before they escalate.

THE IMPORTANCE OF DIGITAL MONITORING

Digital media monitoring gives you a comprehensive view of how your brand or public persona is perceived online. By analyzing data collected from diverse digital sources, including social media, forums, blogs, and news, you can gain valuable insights into audience sentiment, emerging trends, and the performance of your communications campaigns.

DIGITAL MONITORING TOOLS

There are several monitoring tools available on the market, each with its own characteristics and capabilities. Some of the most effective include:

- **Google Alerts** : Setting up Google alerts for your brand name or relevant topics can be a good starting point for monitoring online mentions.

- **Hootsuite** : A social media management platform that allows you to monitor multiple social networks from a single dashboard, making it easy to track relevant conversations and trends.

- **Mention** : Real-time monitoring tool that gives you the ability to track mentions of your brand across the web and social media, allowing you to quickly react to any negative or positive content.

- **Brandwatch** : A more advanced tool that uses artificial intelligence to analyze sentiment and trends around your brand, providing detailed insights that can inform your PR strategy.

EFFECTIVE MONITORING TECHNIQUES

To maximize the effectiveness of your digital media monitoring, consider the following techniques:

- **Defining relevant keywords and topics** : Identify the keywords, phrases, and topics most relevant to your brand or industry. This will help you filter through the noise and focus on the mentions that really matter.

- **Channel segmentation** : Each digital platform has its own culture and type of user. Segmenting your monitoring by channel can help you better understand the nuances of conversations across different platforms.

- **Sentiment analysis** : Use tools that offer sentiment analysis to get a general idea of positive, negative or neutral sentiment towards your brand. This can help prioritize responses and better understand public perception.

- **Reporting and trend analysis** : Create regular reports to analyze trends over time. This not only helps you measure the impact of your PR actions, but also identify emerging opportunities or threats on the digital horizon.

Armed with digital media monitoring tools and techniques, you will be better prepared to manage your online presence and respond proactively to any situation. In the next chapter, " **CRISIS COMMUNICATION IN THE DIGITAL AGE** ," we'll dive into specific strategies for planning and executing effective crisis communications, a critical component to safeguarding your online reputation in times of adversity.

Effective monitoring is your radar in the vast digital ocean, guiding your navigation through the tumultuous waves of online public opinion. Continue your journey with us as we explore how to turn monitoring insights into strategic actions that strengthen your brand in the digital world.

CRISIS COMMUNICATION IN THE DIGITAL AGE

In a world where a single social media post can generate a public relations firestorm, being prepared to communicate effectively during a crisis is more crucial than ever. This chapter covers planning and executing crisis communications in the digital age, providing vital strategies for protecting your online reputation at critical times.

UNDERSTANDING CRISIS COMMUNICATION

Crisis communication refers to the set of strategies and practices employed to deal with negative events or information that have the potential to damage the reputation of a brand or public personality. In the digital environment, where news spreads quickly, a quick and well-articulated response is essential.

ELEMENTS OF AN EFFECTIVE CRISIS COMMUNICATION PLAN

- **Crisis Management Team** : Constitute a team dedicated to crisis management, including members from different departments such as PR, legal and customer service, ensuring a coordinated response.

- **Communication channels** : Determine which channels will be used to communicate during a crisis (e.g. social media, official website, press). Make sure these channels can be quickly updated as needed.

- **Key messages and response templates** : Develop key messages and response templates for potential crisis scenarios. While every crisis requires a personalized approach, having a foundation in place can significantly speed up your response.

- **Monitoring and evaluation protocols** : Establish protocols to monitor the situation in real time and evaluate the effectiveness of your communications. This includes tracking online sentiment and volume of brand mentions.

STRATEGIES FOR COMMUNICATING DURING A CRISIS

- **Quick response** : In the digital environment, time is of the essence. A quick response can help control the narrative before it escalates.

- **Transparency** : Be honest about the situation. Admitting mistakes and communicating the steps being taken to resolve the issue can help rebuild trust.

- **Consistency** : Ensure that all communications, across all channels, are consistent. Contradictory messages can cause confusion and worsen the crisis.

- **Solution focus** : While it is important to acknowledge the problem, communications should focus on the solutions and actions being taken to resolve the crisis.

- **Continuous monitoring** : Keep monitoring the situation and adjust your strategy as necessary. The scenario can change quickly, and flexibility is key.

MOVING FORWARD AFTER THE CRISIS

After the crisis, it is crucial to evaluate the performance of your communications strategy and learn from the experience. Analyze what worked well and what can be improved, adjust your crisis plans based on these insights, and continue to monitor public perception to ensure full reputation recovery.

Now that you are equipped with the strategies for managing crisis communications in the digital age, the next chapter, "**MANAGING CANCELLATION ON SOCIAL MEDIA** ," will explore specific tactics for countering cancellation campaigns and mitigating their effects on social media platforms. These situations, although challenging, offer unique opportunities to reaffirm your brand's values and strengthen your connection with your audience.

Crisis communication is an inevitable part of managing a brand or public image in the digital age. With proper preparation and a strategic approach, you can navigate these moments with confidence and emerge stronger on the other side. Continue your journey with us as we explore how to turn challenges into opportunities for growth and engagement.

MANAGING CANCELLATION ON SOCIAL MEDIA

On social media, where voices are amplified and opinions spread quickly, the phenomenon of cancellation can quickly evolve from a whisper to a deafening roar. This chapter focuses on effective strategies for tackling unsubscribe campaigns on social media platforms, helping you mitigate the impacts and, where possible, turn the tide in favor of your brand or public image.

UNDERSTANDING CANCELLATION ON SOCIAL MEDIA

Cancellation on social media occurs when an individual or brand is the target of widespread criticism, often resulting in a public call to boycott or discredit them. These moves can be triggered by a variety of reasons, from verbal slip-ups to actions considered unethical or offensive.

STRATEGIES TO COPE WITH CANCELLATION

- **Rapid assessment and response** : The first step is to quickly assess the situation to understand the severity of the cancellation and determine the best way to respond. Not all criticism requires a public response, but completely ignoring a significant cancel campaign can be harmful.

- **Transparent and authentic communication** : If a response is necessary, it must be transparent, authentic and aligned with your brand values. Acknowledge the problem, show empathy and, if appropriate, sincerely apologize.

- **Direct and constructive engagement** : Engage directly with the community in a constructive way. This could include responding to specific concerns on social media, holding Q&A sessions, or even organizing virtual meetups to discuss the issue openly.

- **Focus on action** : In addition to words, it is essential to demonstrate through concrete actions that you are committed to making positive changes. This may include reviewing internal policies, implementing training programs, or donating to related causes.

- **Continuous monitoring** : Continue monitoring the situation on social media to assess the effectiveness of your responses and adjust the strategy as necessary. Social media monitoring tools can be valuable here.

RECOVERING FROM A CANCELLATION CAMPAIGN

Recovering from a successful opt-out campaign takes time, patience, and an ongoing commitment to transparency and positive change. Consider these steps to recovery:

- **Post-crisis assessment** : After the storm has passed, carry out a detailed analysis of what happened. Identify what could have been done differently and what was learned.

- **Strategic reconstruction** : Use the insights gained to strengthen your communication strategy on social media, emphasizing authenticity and positive engagement with your audience.

- **Commitment to continuous improvement** : Demonstrate an ongoing commitment to improvement, whether through internal initiatives to promote a more inclusive culture or through external efforts to repair relationships with the community.

Overcoming a social media unsubscribe campaign is just one step in the journey of building and maintaining a strong online reputation. In the next chapter, " **ENGAGEMENT WITH INFLUENCERS** ", we'll explore how collaborating with digital influencers can reinforce your brand's message and build authenticity, helping to prevent future crises and promote a positive image in the long term.

Navigating the turbulent waters of digital cancellation requires not only an effective strategy but also a genuine commitment to change and improvement. Stay with us on this journey as we discover more tools and strategies to strengthen your digital presence in an ever-changing world.

ENGAGEMENT WITH INFLUENCERS

In today's digital landscape, collaborating with influencers has become an indispensable strategy for brands that want to expand their reach, reinforce their message and build authenticity. This chapter explores how strategic engagement with digital influencers can benefit your brand or public image, offering tips for creating fruitful partnerships that advance your public relations goals.

THE POWER OF DIGITAL INFLUENCERS

Digital influencers, with their loyal audiences and specific niches, have the unique ability to shape opinions and trends. They can act as message multipliers for your brand, providing credibility and relevance through their endorsement. The key is to choose influencers whose values and audience align with your brand's.

STRATEGIES FOR EFFECTIVE ENGAGEMENT

- **Influencer identification and selection** : Start by identifying influencers whose niches and values are aligned with your brand. Social media analytics tools can help identify potential candidates based on reach, engagement, and content relevance.

- **Building authentic relationships** : Before proposing a collaboration, invest time building a genuine relationship with influencers. Comment on their posts, share their content, and engage in meaningful ways to make an authentic connection.

- **Personalized proposals** : When you are ready to propose a partnership, do it in a personalized way. Highlight how collaboration can benefit both parties and be open to creative ideas that resonate with the influencer's audience.

- **Establishing clear expectations** : When formalizing the partnership, it is crucial to set clear expectations in terms of deliverables, key messages and brand guidelines. A detailed briefing can help ensure you are both on the same page.

- **Monitoring and evaluation** : Use performance metrics, such as reach, engagement and conversions, to evaluate the success of the partnership. This not only helps you measure ROI but also provides valuable insights for future collaborations.

MAXIMIZING IMPACT

To maximize the impact of engagement with influencers, consider integrating these partnerships into your broader public relations strategy. Cohesive campaigns that combine influencers, organic content, and paid media can significantly amplify your message.

Collaborating with influencers is more than just a marketing strategy; It's a powerful way to build credibility and authenticity in a saturated digital world. In the next chapter, " **SEO FOR PUBLIC RELATIONS** ," we will explore how to optimize your online presence to improve positive visibility and manage online reputation, thus complementing influencer engagement efforts.

In this ever-evolving digital landscape, where authenticity and trust are valuable currencies, leveraging the power of influencers can be the key to strengthening your brand and cultivating lasting relationships with your audience. Join us on this journey as we uncover more strategies to ensure your brand not only survives, but thrives in the digital age.

SEO FOR PUBLIC RELATIONS

In today's digital universe, online visibility is crucial to the success of any brand or public personality. SEO (Search Engine Optimization) is no longer just a digital marketing tool; has become an essential part of public relations strategies. This chapter covers how to use SEO techniques to improve positive visibility and effectively manage online reputation.

INTEGRATING SEO INTO PUBLIC RELATIONS

SEO for PR goes beyond simply optimizing content for search engines. It involves a strategic approach to ensuring that positive messages and branded content are highlighted in search results, while actively managing public perception.

SEO STRATEGIES FOR PR

- **Keywords and key messages** : Identify relevant keywords that your target audience is searching for and incorporate them into your key messages. This includes press releases, blog content, online biographies and other communications materials.

– **Content Optimization** : Make sure all online content is optimized for SEO, including titles, descriptions, header tags, and images. This increases the likelihood of your content being found and ranked positively by search engines.

- **Quality backlinks** : Building backlinks from reputable websites can significantly increase your website's authority in search engines. Collaborations with influencers, media mentions, and guest posts are effective ways to accumulate quality backlinks.

– **Online reputation monitoring** : Use SEO tools to monitor how your brand or name is mentioned online. This allows you to quickly identify negative or false content and take steps to proactively manage it.

– **High-quality content** : Producing high-quality, relevant content is the backbone of SEO. Content that answers your audience's questions and provides value tends to be better ranked and shared, increasing your positive online visibility.

CHALLENGES AND OPPORTUNITIES

The main challenge of SEO for PR is the constant evolution of search algorithms, which requires continuous adaptation and updating of strategies. However, this also presents an opportunity to stay ahead of digital trends by adapting your techniques to ensure maximum visibility and effective online reputation management.

By effectively integrating SEO into your public relations strategies, you can ensure your brand's positive narrative gains prominence in the vast digital world. In the next chapter, " **BRANDED CONTENT AND STORYTELLING** ", we'll dive deeper into the art of telling stories that resonate with your audience, complementing your SEO strategies and further amplifying your online presence.

Employing SEO in public relations is not just about being seen; it's about being seen in the right context. Take this journey with us as we explore how to shape and share the stories that define your brand in the digital age.

BRANDED CONTENT AND STORYTELLING

At the heart of any successful public relations strategy in the digital age is the art of storytelling. Telling engaging and meaningful stories allows brands and public figures to connect emotionally with their audiences, transcending traditional advertising to create lasting bonds. This chapter explores how to integrate branded content and storytelling into your PR strategies, turning every touchpoint into an opportunity to engage and inspire.

THE ESSENCE OF STORYTELLING

Storytelling is more than just telling stories; it's about telling the right story in the right way. Well-told stories have the power to capture imagination, invoke emotions and motivate action. In the context of digital public relations, storytelling becomes a powerful tool to humanize your brand, highlight its values and build credibility.

STORYTELLING STRATEGIES FOR PR

- **Identify your core narrative** : All branded content should revolve around a coherent core narrative. This narrative should reflect your brand's values, mission, and what makes it unique. A well-defined narrative serves as the backbone for all of your stories.

– **Know your audience** : For your stories to resonate, it's critical to understand your audience. What are your interests, concerns and aspirations? Stories that speak directly to the hearts and minds of your audience are the ones that will be remembered and shared.

- **Diversify content format** : Use a variety of content formats to tell your stories, including blogs, videos, podcasts, infographics, and social media. Different formats can capture the attention of different segments of your audience in unique ways.

- **Promote engagement** : Encourage your audience to be

part of your story. This can be done through social media campaigns that invite participation, contests or even content co-creation. Engagement turns passive viewers into active advocates for your brand.

- **Measure impact** : Use analytical tools to evaluate the impact of your stories. Metrics like engagement, shares, comments, and conversions can provide valuable insights into what resonates with your audience.

OVERCOMING CHALLENGES IN STORYTELLING

The biggest challenge in digital storytelling is cutting through the noise. We live in an era of information overload, where the public's attention is highly sought after. To overcome this challenge, your stories need to be not only interesting, but also relevant and delivered at the right time and on the right channel.

As we move into the next chapter, " **MEDIA RELATIONSHIPS IN THE DIGITAL WORLD** ," we will explore how your brand narrative can be amplified through strategic media relationships. Storytelling doesn't end with the content you create; It extends through the stories others tell about you.

By combining effective storytelling techniques with a solid branded content strategy, you can elevate your online presence, deeply engage your audience, and build a lasting reputation in the digital age. Continue on this journey with us as we unlock more tools and strategies to shape public perception and drive your brand's success.

MEDIA RELATIONSHIPS IN THE DIGITAL WORLD

In a constantly evolving digital environment, media relations remain a fundamental pillar of public relations. In this chapter, we'll explore how to cultivate and maintain productive relationships with journalists and media outlets in the digital age, expanding the reach of your brand's narratives and solidifying your online reputation.

THE IMPORTANCE OF SOLID RELATIONSHIPS WITH THE MEDIA

Relationships with the media in the digital world go beyond simply sending press releases. It's about building genuine connections with journalists and media influencers who might be genuinely interested in your story. These relationships can be invaluable during times of crisis or when you need a story to be told accurately and favorably.

STRATEGIES FOR BUILDING MEDIA RELATIONSHIPS

- **Search and personalization** : Start by identifying journalists and media outlets that cover your area of expertise. Understand the type of content they produce and customize your approach based on their interests and needs.

- **Creating valuable content** : Offer exclusive content, expert insights, or early access to important information. Not only does this increase your chances of coverage, it also establishes your brand as a valuable and trustworthy source.

- **Effective communication** : Keep communication clear, concise and relevant. Respect journalists' deadlines and provide all the information necessary to facilitate their work, including quotes, images and contact information.

- **Use of digital platforms** : Take advantage of digital platforms to build and maintain relationships. Following journalists on social media, interacting with their content and sharing their articles can help establish a connection even before the first direct contact.

- **Monitoring and follow-up** : After sending press releases or other information, follow up respectfully to ensure they have received everything they need. After publication, thank and share the content on your own channels.

OVERCOMING CHALLENGES

One of the main challenges in the relationship with digital media is the high competition for attention. To overcome this, it's crucial that your approach stands out, offering unique stories, interesting angles and real value to the media outlet's audience.

Effective media relations are a continuous cycle of research, communication and gratitude. By investing in these relationships, you not only expand the reach of your stories, but also strengthen your brand's position in the digital landscape. In the next chapter, " **STAKEHOLDER MANAGEMENT** ", we'll explore how to identify and manage stakeholder expectations and perceptions, a crucial step in ensuring alignment between your PR strategy and your brand's overall goals.

Media relationships in the digital world are a two-way street, offering benefits for both brands and journalists. Join us on this journey as we continue to explore strategies for cultivating a positive and influential online presence.

STAKEHOLDER MANAGEMENT

Stakeholder management is essential in building and maintaining a positive public image and executing effective public relations strategies. In this chapter, we'll explore how to identify, understand and manage stakeholder expectations and perceptions, ensuring your PR strategies are aligned with brand objectives and meet the needs of everyone involved.

UNDERSTANDING STAKEHOLDERS

Stakeholders are individuals, groups or organizations that have an interest in or are affected by your brand's activities. This includes customers, employees, business partners, investors and the media. Each group has its own expectations and needs, and understanding these differences is crucial to developing effective communications.

STRATEGIES FOR STAKEHOLDER MANAGEMENT

- **Mapping and identification** : The first step is to identify who your stakeholders are and map their level of influence and interest in relation to your brand. This helps prioritize communication efforts and customize messages.

- **Understanding needs** : Understanding the needs, concerns and expectations of each group of stakeholders is vital. This can be achieved through surveys, interviews or feedback sessions.

- **Effective communication** : Develop a communication plan that addresses the specific needs of each stakeholder group. Communication must be clear, consistent and regular to build trust and maintain positive relationships.

- **Proactive engagement** : Involve stakeholders in decisions and processes that affect them. Not only does this demonstrate respect for their opinions, but it can also provide valuable insights to improve your PR strategies.

- **Monitoring and adjustments** : Continuously monitor

stakeholder insights and feedback, and be ready to adjust your strategies as needed. Stakeholder management is a dynamic process that requires flexibility and adaptability.

OVERCOMING CHALLENGES

One of the biggest challenges in stakeholder management is balancing conflicting interests. Effective communication and the search for win-win solutions are essential to overcome these obstacles and maintain harmonious relationships.

Effective stakeholder management is a crucial component of any successful public relations strategy. It allows you to build a solid foundation of support, minimize conflicts and maximize cooperation between everyone involved. In the next chapter, "**TRANSPARENCY AND AUTHENTICITY** ", we will explore how these values can be incorporated into your PR strategies to further strengthen your public image and the trust of your stakeholders.

Understanding and managing stakeholder expectations not only strengthens your brand image, but also contributes to the long-term success of your PR initiatives. Stay with us on this journey as we uncover strategies for building and maintaining positive relationships in today's volatile digital environment.

TRANSPARENCY AND AUTHENTICITY

Transparency and authenticity are more than just buzzwords in the world of public relations; they are critical foundations for building trust and loyalty with your stakeholders in an increasingly skeptical digital environment. This chapter explores the importance of integrating transparency and authenticity into your PR strategies, providing guidance on how these values can be communicated effectively to strengthen your public image.

THE IMPORTANCE OF TRANSPARENCY AND AUTHENTICITY

In a world full of information and choices, consumers and other stakeholders value brands that are open, honest and genuine. Transparency is not just about disclosing information; it's about being open about your practices, successes and, equally important, your failures. Authenticity goes beyond maintaining an image; it's about aligning your actions with your stated values, ensuring your brand "practices what it preaches."

COMMUNICATING TRANSPARENCY AND AUTHENTICITY

- **Real stories, real people** : Use your communications platforms to tell real stories involving your team, customers or partners. These stories should honestly reflect your brand's values and culture.

- **Open dialogue** : Encourage and participate in open conversations with your stakeholders, whether through social media, forums or live events. Be willing to discuss sensitive issues respectfully and constructively.

- **Admitting errors** : When errors occur, take responsibility promptly. Explain what went wrong, what is being done to correct the problem, and how future errors will be prevented.

- **Feedback and action** : Demonstrate how feedback from stakeholders influences your decisions and actions. This not only validates the importance of your contributions, but also reinforces your authenticity.

- **Consistency in communication** : Ensure your messages are consistent across all channels. Inconsistencies can undermine trust and question your authenticity.

BENEFITS OF BEING TRANSPARENT AND AUTHENTIC

Adopting a transparent and authentic approach can bring numerous benefits, including a strengthened public reputation, a loyal customer base, and the ability to attract and retain talent. Furthermore, in times of crisis, brands that have already established a reputation for transparency and authenticity tend to recover more quickly.

OVERCOMING CHALLENGES

One of the biggest challenges is balancing transparency with the need to protect sensitive information. The key is to communicate openly as much as possible, while clearly explaining the reasons for keeping certain information private.

Integrating transparency and authenticity into your PR strategies is not only beneficial; It's essential in today's digital age. In the next chapter, " **VISUAL CONTENT STRATEGIES** ," we'll explore how to utilize visual content to reinforce your PR messages, engaging your audience in an effective and memorable way.

Building a strong brand in the digital age requires more than just an online presence; it requires creating a genuine connection with your stakeholders. Continue on this journey with us as we explore ways to communicate your brand values effectively by leveraging the power of transparency and authenticity.

VISUAL CONTENT STRATEGIES

In a digital world saturated with information, visual content emerges as a powerful way to capture the public's attention, communicate complex messages quickly and effectively, and reinforce brand identity and values. This chapter addresses the importance of visual content in public relations strategies and provides guidelines for creating visuals that engage and inspire your audience.

THE POWER OF VISUAL CONTENT

Visual content — including images, videos, infographics, and motion graphics — has the unique ability to convey emotion, tell stories, and present information in a quick, digestible way. In the context of PR, strategically using visual content can significantly amplify the impact of your communications, making them more memorable and shareable.

DEVELOPING EFFECTIVE VISUAL CONTENT STRATEGIES

- **Alignment with brand message** : Make sure all visual content reflects and reinforces your brand message and values. Visual consistency helps build recognition and trust.

- **Quality over quantity** : Invest in high-quality visual content. Attractive, professional visuals elevate your brand's perception and better capture your audience's attention.

- **Format diversification** : Explore different visual content formats to keep your audience engaged. Videos, lives, social media stories, infographics and high-quality photos can meet different preferences and information needs.

- **Optimization for platforms** : Adapt and optimize your visual content for each social media platform, considering the specificities and limitations of each one. This maximizes the impact and visibility of your visuals.

- **Storytelling integration** : Use visual content to tell stories that resonate emotionally with your audience. Visual stories can be especially effective for conveying brand missions, social impact, or customer stories.

- Interactivity and engagement : Consider creating interactive visual content, such as quizzes, polls or games, to increase engagement. Interactivity can also provide valuable insights into your audience's preferences.

MEASURING SUCCESS

To evaluate the effectiveness of your visual content strategies, monitor metrics such as engagement, shares, comments, and conversions. This information can help you refine your approaches and identify the types of content that resonate most with your audience.

OVERCOMING CHALLENGES

One of the challenges of visual content is keeping the production of materials fresh and relevant, which can require significant resources. Collaborating with content creators, utilizing accessible design tools, and leveraging user-generated content can be effective strategies for overcoming these barriers.

With visual content strategies well implemented, you are ready to capture your audience's attention in a powerful and memorable way. In the next chapter, " **DIGITAL RIGHTS AND ONLINE ETHICS** ," we'll explore how to navigate copyright and ethics issues in online communications, ensuring that your visual content not only engages, but also respects legal and ethical standards.

Visual content is an indispensable tool in the arsenal of any modern public relations strategy, offering a powerful means to tell your story and connect with your audience. Continue this journey with us as we explore more crucial aspects of strengthening your digital presence and online reputation.

DIGITAL RIGHTS AND ONLINE ETHICS

Navigating the complexities of digital rights and online ethics is essential for brands and public figures seeking to maintain responsible communications practices in the digital age. This chapter discusses the importance of understanding and respecting copyright and online ethics, providing guidance to ensure that your visual content and public relations strategies comply with laws and ethical standards.

UNDERSTANDING DIGITAL RIGHTS AND ONLINE ETHICS

Digital rights refer to intellectual property rights applied to the digital environment, including copyrights to images, videos, texts and other creative content. Online ethics, in turn, addresses correct and fair practices in the use and sharing of content on the internet, ensuring that online actions respect both individual and collective rights.

PRACTICES TO RESPECT DIGITAL RIGHTS AND ONLINE ETHICS

- **Use of licensed and original content** : Whenever possible, create your own visual content or use images, videos and music licensed through reputable image banks or under Creative Commons licenses suitable for commercial use.

- **Proper attribution** : When using third-party content, provide clear and accurate attribution as specified by the creator or the license under which the content is made available.

- **Respect for privacy and consent** : Obtain clear consent before using personal images or stories in your PR campaigns, especially in contexts that may be sensitive or personal.

- **Transparency in advertising and partnerships** : Be transparent about paid partnerships or sponsored content, using hashtags such as #publi or #ad to indicate that it is an advertising communication.

- **Fact-checking and accountability** : Ensure all content shared is accurate and fact-checked, preventing the spread of false or misleading information.

NAVIGATING LEGAL AND ETHICAL CHALLENGES

Copyright infringement and online ethics can result in serious legal consequences and damage your brand's reputation. Stay informed about copyright laws and best ethical practices, and consider consulting with knowledgeable legal professionals when necessary.

Respecting digital rights and online ethics not only protects your brand against legal and ethical risks, but also builds trust with your audience, reinforcing your reputation as a responsible and upstanding brand. In the next chapter, " **EMERGING TECHNOLOGIES IN PR** ," we'll explore how new technologies like AI and blockchain are redefining public relations strategies, opening up new possibilities for communication and engagement.

In this constantly evolving digital environment, it is crucial that brands and public figures navigate carefully and responsibly, ensuring that their communications strategies reflect not only their goals, but also a commitment to fair and ethical practices. Stay with us on this journey as we discover how to ethically and effectively integrate emerging technologies into your PR strategies.

EMERGING TECHNOLOGIES IN PR

As the field of public relations continues to evolve, incorporating emerging technologies has become a crucial strategy for brands and personalities looking to innovate their communications and engagement with the public. This chapter explores the impact of Artificial Intelligence (AI), blockchain, augmented reality (AR), and other technologies on reinventing PR strategies, highlighting how these tools can be used to improve communication and data analysis.

ARTIFICIAL INTELLIGENCE (AI) IN PR

AI is transforming PR in many ways, from automating repetitive tasks to personalizing communication with the public. AI-based tools can analyze large volumes of data to identify trends and patterns, allowing brands to anticipate audience needs and personalize their messages more effectively. Additionally, AI-powered chatbots can provide real-time customer service, improving user experience.

BLOCKCHAIN FOR TRANSPARENCY AND SECURITY

Blockchain is beginning to be explored in PR to improve the transparency and security of communication. This technology can be used to verify the authenticity of documents and releases, ensuring that the information shared is reliable and unaltered. This is particularly relevant in a scenario where trust in the media and institutions is declining.

AUGMENTED REALITY (AR) AND IMMERSIVE EXPERIENCES

AR offers new opportunities for brands to create immersive and engaging experiences, allowing the public to interact with products or services virtually before purchasing. PR campaigns that incorporate AR can significantly increase engagement, providing users with a deeper, more tangible understanding of the brand's offering.

CHALLENGES AND ETHICAL CONSIDERATIONS

Despite their potential, implementing emerging technologies in PR comes with challenges and ethical considerations. Data privacy is a primary concern, especially with the use of AI and data analytics. Brands must ensure transparency in how data is collected and used, as well as comply with data protection regulations such as GDPR in Europe. Furthermore, it is crucial to maintain a balance between automation and human interaction, preserving the authenticity of communication.

As we move into the next chapter, " **DATA ANALYSIS IN PR** ," we will explore how data analytics, supported by emerging technologies, can provide valuable insights for optimizing PR strategies and measuring the impact of campaigns. Emerging technologies offer powerful tools to innovate and improve public relations, but their success depends on careful implementation and ethical consideration.

The integration of emerging technologies into PR strategies represents an exciting frontier of innovation and personalization. However, to maximize its potential, it is critical to address the associated challenges and ethical considerations. Stay with us on this journey as we uncover how to harness the power of data analytics to transform your public relations.

DATA ANALYSIS IN PR

Data analysis has become an indispensable tool for public relations professionals, enabling a deeper understanding of the impact of their strategies and the optimization of future campaigns based on concrete insights. This chapter explores how data analytics can be effectively applied to PR, highlighting best practices for collecting, interpreting, and acting on data.

THE POWER OF DATA ANALYSIS IN PR

Data analysis allows you to measure the success of PR initiatives in a quantitative way, offering a clear view of the return on investment (ROI) and effectiveness of campaigns. Additionally, insights generated by data analysis can help identify market trends, audience preferences, content performance and media reach, enabling strategic adjustments that improve future communications.

IMPLEMENTING DATA ANALYSIS INTO PR STRATEGIES

- **Defining clear objectives** : Before starting data collection, it is essential to define what you want to achieve with your analysis. This could include increasing brand visibility, audience engagement, or message effectiveness.

- **Data collection** : Utilize a variety of tools and platforms to collect relevant data. This can include social media analytics, media monitoring tools, audience surveys, and website traffic data.

- **Analysis and interpretation** : Analyze collected data to identify patterns, trends and insights. Interpreting data requires an understanding of PR objectives and how they relate to observed results.

- **Data-driven action** : Use insights gained to inform and adjust your PR strategies. This may include optimizing content, retargeting audiences, or changing communication channels.

- **Continuous measurement and adjustment** : Data analysis is a continuous process. Regularly evaluate the impact of implemented changes and be ready to make additional adjustments based on new data and insights.

CHALLENGES IN DATA ANALYSIS

One of the main challenges in data analysis in PR is ensuring the quality and relevance of the data collected. Furthermore, interpreting data effectively requires specific skills and understanding of the PR context. Overcoming these challenges often requires ongoing training and, in some cases, collaboration with data analytics experts.

Data analysis offers PR professionals the opportunity to make informed, evidence-based decisions, increasing the impact and efficiency of their strategies. In the next chapter, " **ONLINE FEEDBACK MANAGEMENT** ," we'll explore how to collect, interpret, and respond to online feedback constructively, a crucial step in continually improving and maintaining positive relationships with the public.

In an increasingly data-driven digital environment, the ability to interpret and act on accurate information is critical to the success of PR strategies. Continue this journey with us as we explore advanced techniques for managing online feedback and strengthening your digital presence.

ONLINE FEEDBACK MANAGEMENT

Online feedback has become an invaluable source of insights for brands and public figures, offering direct insight into audience perceptions, experiences and expectations. This chapter covers how to collect, interpret, and respond to online feedback effectively, turning it into a powerful tool for continuous improvement and strengthening relationships with your audience.

THE IMPORTANCE OF ONLINE FEEDBACK

Online feedback, whether through social media comments, website reviews or discussion forums, provides real data on the public's reaction to your PR initiatives. In addition to measuring satisfaction and capturing suggestions for improvements, online feedback allows you to quickly identify possible crises and adjust communication strategies as necessary.

STRATEGIES FOR ONLINE FEEDBACK MANAGEMENT

- **Active monitoring** : Use social media monitoring tools and other digital platforms to collect feedback on an ongoing basis. This includes brand mentions, relevant hashtags, and discussions around the themes associated with your image.

- **Analysis and interpretation** : Evaluate collected feedback to identify trends, recurring problems and opportunities for improvement. Sentiment analysis can be particularly useful for understanding the emotional nature of feedback.

- **Quick and personalized response** : Responding quickly and personalized to feedback, especially when it is negative, demonstrates that your brand values the public's opinions and is committed to resolving potential problems.

- **Integrating feedback into PR strategies** : Use the insights gained from feedback to adjust and improve your PR strategies. This may include changes in communication, adapting products or services, and reviewing customer service practices.

- **Sharing learnings and improvements** : When actions are taken based on feedback, share these improvements with your audience. This not only closes the feedback loop, but also reinforces the perception of a thoughtful and evolving brand.

OVERCOMING CHALLENGES

One of the challenges in managing online feedback is dealing with the significant volume of data and identifying which feedback requires immediate action. Additionally, responding appropriately to negative reviews or emotionally charged feedback requires sensitivity and a deep understanding of the context.

Effective online feedback management is fundamental to any modern public relations strategy, serving as a direct bridge between the brand and its audience. In the next chapter, "**PREVENTING DIGITAL CRISES** ", we will explore how to use insights gained from online feedback to prevent potential crises, further strengthening your brand's resilience and reputation in the digital environment.

By approaching online feedback not as an obligation, but as an opportunity for growth and improvement, brands and public figures can develop a deeper, more meaningful relationship with their audience. Continue this journey with us, as we unveil proactive strategies for managing digital crises and preserving the integrity of your online image.

PREVENTING DIGITAL CRISES

Preventing digital crises is an essential component of protecting the reputation of brands and public figures online. This chapter offers a look at how to identify potential risks and implement proactive strategies to prevent them from turning into crises, using insights gained from online feedback and other data analysis.

IDENTIFYING POTENTIAL RISKS

- **Continuous monitoring** : Utilize monitoring tools to track brand mentions, industry trends, and relevant discussions. This allows you to identify potential warning signs before they turn into crises.

– **Sentiment Analysis** : Employ sentiment analysis to understand the emotions behind your brand mentions. Negative spikes in sentiment can indicate emerging issues that need attention.

- **Feedback and reviews** : Pay attention to customer feedback and reviews of products or services. Recurring criticisms in specific areas may be indicative of larger problems.

CRISIS PREVENTION STRATEGIES

- **Crisis plan** : Develop and maintain an up-to-date crisis management plan, including rapid response protocols, emergency contact list and communication templates.

- **Internal communication** : Ensure that the team is well informed about communication policies and procedures in the event of a crisis. Regular training can help prepare your team to respond effectively.

- **Proactive transparency** : Be transparent about challenges or potentially controversial changes. Proactively communicating about such issues can help control the narrative and reduce the likelihood of misunderstandings.

- **Engagement with stakeholders** : Maintain an open

dialogue with important stakeholders, including customers, partners and the media. This can help build robust support that can be vital in times of crisis.

- **Crisis simulations** : Conduct crisis simulations to test the effectiveness of your crisis management plan and identify areas for improvement.

OVERCOMING CHALLENGES

The challenge in preventing digital crises lies in the unpredictable nature of the online environment. The speed at which information can spread requires constant vigilance and the ability to respond quickly. Staying informed about digital trends and proactively adjusting your strategies are crucial steps to mitigating risk.

Implementing a solid crisis prevention strategy can not only save your brand's reputation, but also reinforce your audience's trust and loyalty. In the next chapter, " **SPOKESKEEP TRAINING** ", we will explore how to prepare your brand spokespeople to effectively communicate your brand message, especially in times of crisis, ensuring consistency and clarity in communication.

Taking a proactive approach to digital risk management allows brands and public figures to navigate the online environment with confidence, transforming potential threats into opportunities to strengthen their digital presence and reputation. Stay with us on this journey as we delve deeper into developing crucial skills for effective crisis management.

SPOKESKEEP TRAINING

Spokesperson training is a key component in the communications strategy of any brand or public figure, especially crucial in times of crisis. This chapter focuses on how to effectively prepare spokespeople to communicate your brand message coherently and effectively, ensuring that communication positively reinforces your brand image in all circumstances.

THE IMPORTANCE OF WELL PREPARED SPOKESPERSONS

Spokespeople are the face and voice of your brand; they play a vital role in how the brand is perceived by the public. A well-prepared spokesperson can not only convey the brand's message clearly and convincingly, but can also help navigate the brand through crises, minimizing potential reputational damage.

SPOKESKEEP TRAINING STRATEGIES

- **Judicious selection** : Choose spokespeople who not only have exceptional communication skills, but who also deeply understand the brand's mission, values and policies.

- **Comprehensive training** : Provide comprehensive training that covers everything from branding fundamentals to advanced communication and crisis management techniques. This should include mock interviews and crisis scenarios.

- **Key messages** : Develop and reinforce key messages that reflect the brand's values and objectives. Make sure spokespeople are familiar with these messages and able to incorporate them naturally into communication.

- **Answers to difficult questions** : Prepare spokespeople to handle difficult questions by providing them with pre-written answers to potentially complicated or controversial questions.

- **Update and recycling** : Keep spokespeople up to date with the latest information and trends related to the brand and industry. Hold training sessions regularly to refresh skills and adjust strategies as needed.

OVERCOMING CHALLENGES

One of the biggest challenges in training spokespeople is ensuring they remain authentic while communicating brand messages. Encourage spokespeople to adapt key messages to their own communication style, while remaining consistent with the brand's image and values.

Well-prepared spokespersons are fundamental to the effectiveness of public relations strategies, capable of positively influencing public perception at critical moments. In the next chapter, " **MULTI-CHANNEL NARRATIVES** ," we'll explore how to integrate PR messaging across multiple digital and traditional channels to ensure cohesive, broad-based brand communication.

The preparation and continuous training of spokespeople reinforces the brand's resilience and credibility, especially in times of crisis. Continue this journey with us as we dive deeper into strategies for maximizing the impact of your communications across a diverse media ecosystem.

MULTI-CHANNEL NARRATIVES

In an increasingly fragmented media ecosystem, taking a multi-channel approach to public relations strategies is essential to effectively reach and engage your target audience. This chapter explores how to synchronize and adapt PR messages across multiple digital and traditional channels, creating a cohesive narrative that reinforces your brand image and expands your reach.

THE IMPORTANCE OF A MULTICHANNEL STRATEGY

Multichannel communication allows brands to meet their audience where they are, whether on social media, blogs, email, traditional media or live events. A well-executed strategy ensures that the brand message is consistent across all touchpoints, but adapted to fit the specifics of each channel.

DEVELOPING MULTICHANNEL NARRATIVES

- **Channel mapping** : Identify which channels are most relevant to your audience. This includes an analysis of where your audience spends time online and what content formats they prefer.

- **Unified message, diverse formats** : Develop a unified core message that can be adapted and distributed across different channels. Each adaptation must take into account the format and conventions of the specific channel.

- **Coordinated schedule** : Plan a launch schedule that coordinates the dissemination of messages across all selected channels. This helps build momentum and reinforce the message through strategic repetition.

- **Feedback integration** : Use feedback received in one channel to inform and adjust communication in others. This creates a dynamic feedback loop that can increase the overall effectiveness of the campaign.

- **Measure and adjust** : Monitor performance across channels and be ready to adjust your strategy as needed. Analytics tools can provide valuable insights into the reach and reception of your message.

OVERCOMING CHALLENGES

Managing multichannel storytelling can be challenging, especially when it comes to maintaining message consistency while adapting to different channels. Effective communication within the team and the use of a shared editorial calendar are key to ensuring that all members are aligned and that messages are cohesive and synchronized.

Adopting a multichannel storytelling strategy not only expands the reach of your message, but also reinforces your brand identity through consistent and tailored communication. In the next chapter, "**PR AND CORPORATE SOCIAL RESPONSIBILITY (CSR)**", we'll explore how to align your PR strategies with CSR initiatives to further reinforce your positive brand image.

Implementing an effective multichannel approach requires careful planning, precise execution, and flexibility to adapt to changes in the media environment. Stay with us on this journey as we explore how to integrate corporate social responsibility into your public relations strategies to create a lasting positive impact.

PR AND CORPORATE SOCIAL RESPONSIBILITY (CSR)

Integrating Corporate Social Responsibility (CSR) into public relations strategies is more than a trend — it's a necessity for brands looking to create a positive impact and strengthen their reputation over the long term. This chapter explores how to align your PR initiatives with CSR efforts, highlighting how this synergy can reinforce brand image and promote meaningful engagement with the public and society as a whole.

THE IMPORTANCE OF CSR IN PR STRATEGIES

Incorporating CSR into PR strategies not only demonstrates the brand's commitment to social, environmental and governance issues, but also helps build trust and credibility with stakeholders. By communicating CSR initiatives effectively, brands can highlight their values, differentiate themselves in the marketplace, and foster a deeper connection with their audiences.

STRATEGIES TO INTEGRATE CSR AND PR

- **Identification of aligned causes** : Select CSR initiatives that are aligned with your brand's values and your audience's expectations. This ensures authenticity and relevance in your communications.

- **Clear and transparent communication** : Communicate your CSR actions clearly and transparently. Use real stories and measurable results to demonstrate the impact of your initiatives.

- **Public engagement** : Encourage public engagement in your CSR initiatives. This could include interactive campaigns, partnerships with NGOs, or community events that allow the public to actively participate.

- **Strategic partnerships** : Establish partnerships with organizations that share similar values and that can amplify your CSR messages. This can expand the reach and effectiveness of your initiatives.

- **Progress monitoring and reporting** : Monitor the progress of your CSR initiatives and communicate that progress regularly to your audience. Sustainability reports and frequent updates can help maintain transparency and reinforce brand commitment.

OVERCOMING CHALLENGES

One of the main challenges when integrating CSR into PR strategies is ensuring that actions are not perceived as an attempt at "greenwashing" or superficial promotion. To overcome this, it is crucial that CSR initiatives are genuine, well-planned and aligned with the brand's core values.

The successful integration of CSR and PR not only benefits society, but also positively reinforces brand reputation, contributing to long-term success. In the next chapter, " **PR STRATEGIES FOR STARTUPS** ", we will explore specific public relations approaches for startups in a volatile digital environment, emphasizing how CSR principles can be incorporated from the beginning.

Taking a responsible, socially conscious approach to public relations is a powerful competitive differentiator that can boost customer loyalty and promote a positive brand image. Stay with us on this journey as we uncover specific strategies for startups to effectively engage their audiences by aligning themselves with responsible and sustainable practices.

PR STRATEGIES FOR STARTUPS

Startups operate in a unique environment, characterized by rapid change, limited resources and the need to stand out in a competitive market. Integrating effective public relations (PR) strategies is crucial to building your brand, gaining visibility and attracting investment. This chapter addresses specific PR approaches for startups, highlighting the importance of incorporating Corporate Social Responsibility (CSR) practices from the beginning.

UNDERSTANDING THE PR LANDSCAPE FOR STARTUPS

For startups, PR is not just about generating media coverage; it's about telling the story of your innovation, building credibility and establishing trusting relationships with stakeholders, including customers, investors and the wider community. CSR initiatives can reinforce these goals, demonstrating the startup's commitment to broader values beyond profit.

EFFECTIVE PR STRATEGIES FOR STARTUPS

- **Authentic narrative** : Develop a strong, authentic narrative that captures the essence of your startup — the problem it solves, its mission, and what sets it apart. Stories that incorporate elements of CSR can resonate more deeply with audiences.

- **Focus on relationships** : Build strategic relationships with journalists, bloggers and influencers who align with your startup's niche. Personalized communications and offering unique insights can increase your chances of gaining significant coverage.

- **Leveraging social media** : Use social media to amplify your message, engage directly with the public and show the impact of your CSR initiatives. Social platforms offer a dynamic, low-cost way to share updates, success stories and attract a community around your brand.

- **Events and partnerships** : Participating in industry events, conferences and webinars can increase your startup's visibility. Partnering with organizations that share similar CSR values can also amplify your brand's reach and strengthen its message.

- **Measurement and adaptation** : Monitor the impact of your PR strategies and adjust as necessary. Digital analytics tools can help assess audience engagement, media reach and return on investment in PR activities.

OVERCOMING CHALLENGES

One of the biggest challenges for startups is to stand out in a saturated market. Focusing on a unique story, leveraging specific niches, and maintaining authenticity can help overcome this hurdle. Furthermore, integrating CSR practices from the beginning can differentiate the startup, attracting customers and investors who value social responsibility.

For startups, a well-planned PR strategy that includes a strong CSR component can be decisive for success. In the next chapter, " **PR CAMPAIGN DEVELOPMENT** ," we'll dive into how to plan and execute PR campaigns that resonate in both the digital age and traditional environments, ensuring your startup not only captures attention but also builds a lasting legacy.

Adopting innovative PR approaches and incorporating CSR can help startups build a strong brand, establish market credibility, and make a positive impact on society. Continue on this journey with us as we explore how to develop and implement PR campaigns that make a difference.

PR CAMPAIGN DEVELOPMENT

Developing effective public relations (PR) campaigns is crucial for any organization looking to increase its visibility, build a positive reputation, and meaningfully engage with its audience. This chapter focuses on planning and executing PR campaigns that align digital and traditional strategies, maximizing impact and achieving long-term strategic objectives.

PR CAMPAIGN PLANNING

Effective planning is the backbone of any successful PR campaign. It involves clearly defining objectives, identifying the target audience, creating key messages and choosing the most appropriate communication channels to achieve your objectives.

- **Setting objectives** : Establish what the campaign aims to achieve, whether that's increases in brand visibility, improvements in reputation or improved audience engagement.

- **Target Audience Identification** : Understand who you are trying to reach with your campaign. A clear understanding of your audience allows you to create messages that resonate and choose the most effective channels for communication.

- **Development of key messages** : Create clear and impactful messages that effectively communicate the value of your brand or initiative. Messages must be adaptable for different channels, but consistent at their core.

- **Channel selection** : Determine the communication channels that will be used, from social media and blogs to traditional media and events. The selection should reflect where your target audience consumes information.

EXECUTING PR CAMPAIGNS

Running a PR campaign involves coordinating distribution of your messages across selected channels, continually monitoring performance, and adapting strategies as needed.

- **Coordinated launch** : Ensure all campaign elements are launched in a coordinated and timely manner to maximize impact.

- **Engagement and interaction** : Stay engaged with your audience during the campaign, responding to feedback and adapting your communication according to the public's reaction.

- **Monitoring and evaluation** : Use analytics tools to monitor campaign performance in real time, allowing for quick adjustments to optimize results.

MEASURING SUCCESS

Evaluating the success of a PR campaign must be based on the initial objectives established. Metrics such as media coverage, social media engagement, increased website traffic, and changes in brand perception can provide valuable insights into the impact of the campaign.

Developing and executing successful PR campaigns requires careful planning, skillful execution and the ability to quickly adapt to changes in the media environment. In the next chapter, " **THE FUTURE OF DIGITAL PUBLIC RELATIONS** ," we'll explore emerging trends and projections for how PR strategies will continue to evolve in the digital future.

Well-planned and executed PR campaigns can significantly transform a brand's visibility and reputation. Continue this journey with us as we look to the future and anticipate how to adapt and innovate PR strategies to stay relevant and impactful in the ever-changing digital landscape.

THE FUTURE OF DIGITAL PUBLIC RELATIONS

As we move into an increasingly digitalized future, public relations faces significant transformations, driven by technological innovation, changes in media consumption habits and the growing demand for transparency and authenticity. This chapter explores emerging trends and projections for how PR strategies can evolve, adapting to continue to create significant impact.

EMERGING TRENDS IN DIGITAL PR

- **Artificial intelligence and automation** : AI will continue to reshape PR, offering new tools for content personalization, predictive analytics and real-time monitoring, enabling more targeted and efficient campaigns.

- **Augmented and virtual reality** : Immersive technologies offer new ways to engage audiences, from branded experiences to simulations that allow audiences to "experience" products or services before launch.

- **Direct communication and messaging platforms** : Direct communication with the public through messaging platforms and social applications will gain even more relevance, demanding a more personalized and conversational approach to PR.

- **Ethics and transparency** : In a digital environment where trust can be easily undermined, the emphasis on ethical and transparent practices will become even more critical, with brands being held accountable for their actions and communications.

- **Sustainability and social responsibility** : The demand for sustainable practices and corporate social responsibility will continue to grow, with CSR becoming an integral component of PR strategies.

PREPARING FOR THE FUTURE

To successfully navigate this dynamic future, brands will need to:

- **Adopt emerging technologies** : Stay up to date on the latest innovations and be ready to integrate them into your PR strategies.

- **Focus on authenticity** : Cultivate an authentic brand voice and ensure all communications reflect your true values.

- **Prioritize audience engagement** : Develop strategies that promote meaningful engagement, using data and feedback to personalize interactions.

- **Strengthen flexibility and resilience** : Be prepared to quickly adapt strategies in response to changes in the digital environment and public expectations.

Digital public relations is on the cusp of an era of unprecedented innovation, where creativity, technology and ethics intertwine to define the next generation of brand communications. As we wrap up this comprehensive guide to the evolution of public relations in the digital age, it's important to reflect on the transformations that continue to reshape the field of PR and how professionals, brands, and public figures can adapt and thrive in this ever-changing landscape.

THE IMPORTANCE OF CONTINUOUS ADAPTATION

If there is a recurring theme in this book, it is the need for continuous adaptation. The digital world is constantly evolving, as are public expectations. PR professionals must remain agile, willing to learn and adapt to new technologies, trends and audience behaviors to keep their strategies effective and relevant.

IMPLEMENTATION OF THE DISCUSSED STRATEGIES

We encourage readers to implement the strategies discussed in this book into their PR practices. This includes not only adopting emerging tools and technologies, but also cultivating a culture of transparency, authenticity and social responsibility, crucial elements for building and maintaining public trust in the digital age.

LOOKING TO THE FUTURE

The future of digital public relations is bright and full of opportunities for those who embrace change. As we continue to ride the waves of digital innovation, remember that the heart of PR remains the same: building and maintaining positive relationships. The tools and platforms may change, but the essence of meaningfully connecting with your audience will always be at the heart of effective public relations.

This book is just the beginning of your journey. The field of public relations will continue to evolve, and we hope the strategies and insights shared here serve as a trusted guide as you explore the dynamic world of digital PR. Be curious, be bold and, above all, be prepared to adapt and innovate.

Thank you for accompanying us on this journey through Press Office 3.0. Together, we will continue to shape the future of digital public relations by creating authentic connections, building resilient reputations and making a positive impact in the digital world.

As we turn the final page of this journey together, I sincerely hope that the learnings shared here have touched your heart and sparked new perspectives. If this book has brought you any value, I kindly ask that you take a few moments to leave a review on Amazon. Your words not only help me grow and hone my craft, but they also guide other readers in their quests for knowledge and inspiration. Your opinion is a valuable gift, both for me and for the community of readers looking for stories that transform. I sincerely thank you for sharing this journey with me and I hope we can meet again in the pages of a new adventure.

REGINALDO OSNILDO

Hello, I'm Reginaldo Osnildo, author and innovator in the areas of sales, technology, and communication strategies. My experience ranges from the academic environment, as a professor and researcher at the University of Southern Santa Catarina, to practice as a strategist at Grupo Catarinense de Rádios. With a PhD in sales narratives and digital convergence, and a master's degree in storytelling and social imaginary, I bring my readers a unique fusion of theory and practice. My goal is to provide knowledge in a simple, practical and didactic language, encouraging direct application in personal and professional life.

Yours sincerely

Reginaldo Osnildo

+55 48 991913865

reginaldoosnildo@gmail.com

www.ingramcontent.com/pod-product-compliance
Lightning Source LLC
Chambersburg PA
CBHW070348230526
45471CB00006B/2474